It is Sid.

2

Sid can dip in it.
What is it?

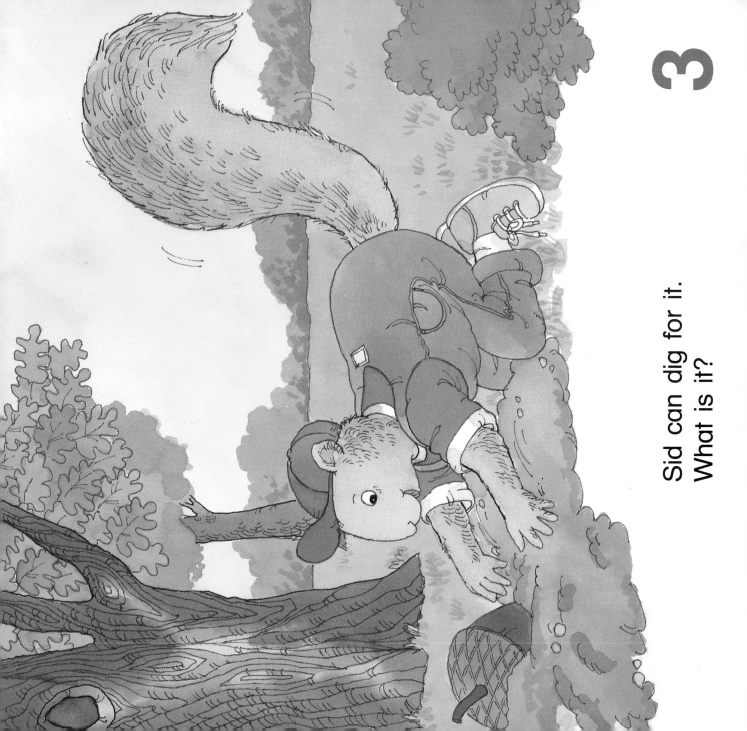

Sid can dig for it.
What is it?

4

Sid can fill it.
What is it?

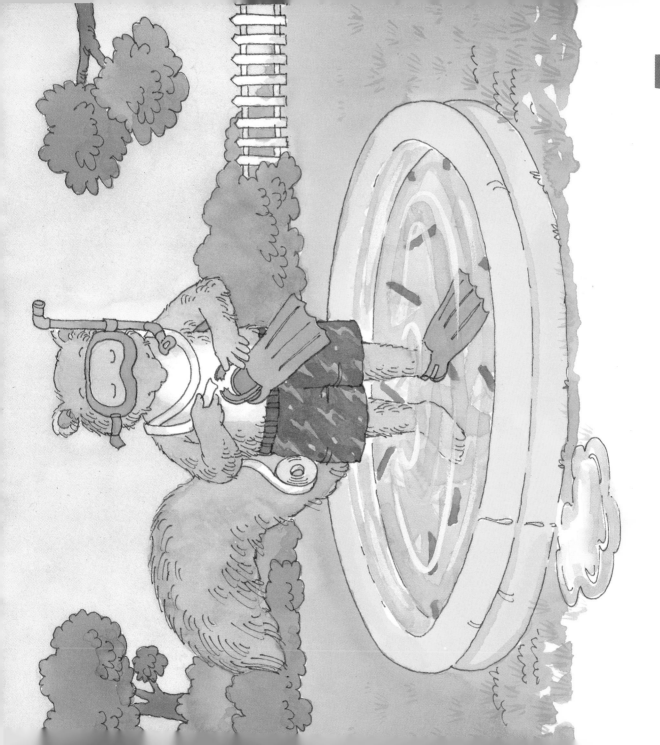

5

Sid can fix it.
What is it?

6

Sid can sit in it.
What is it?

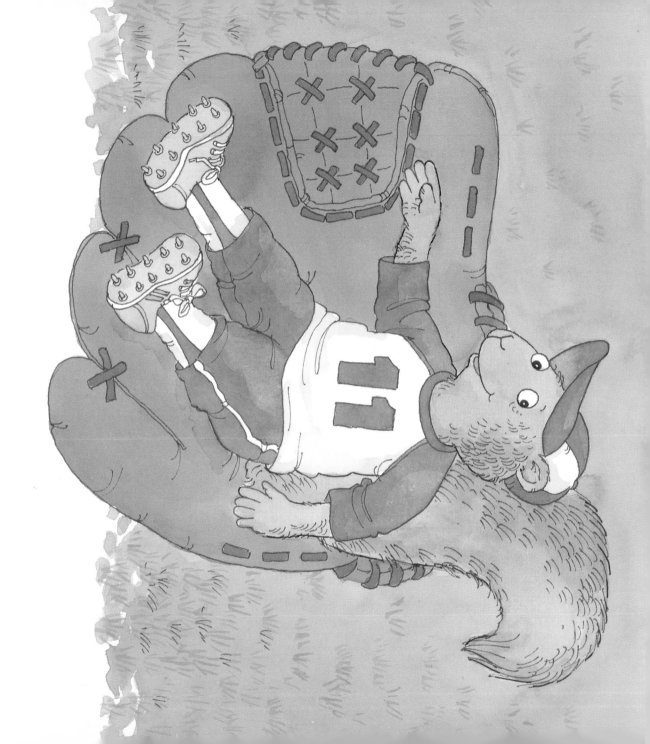

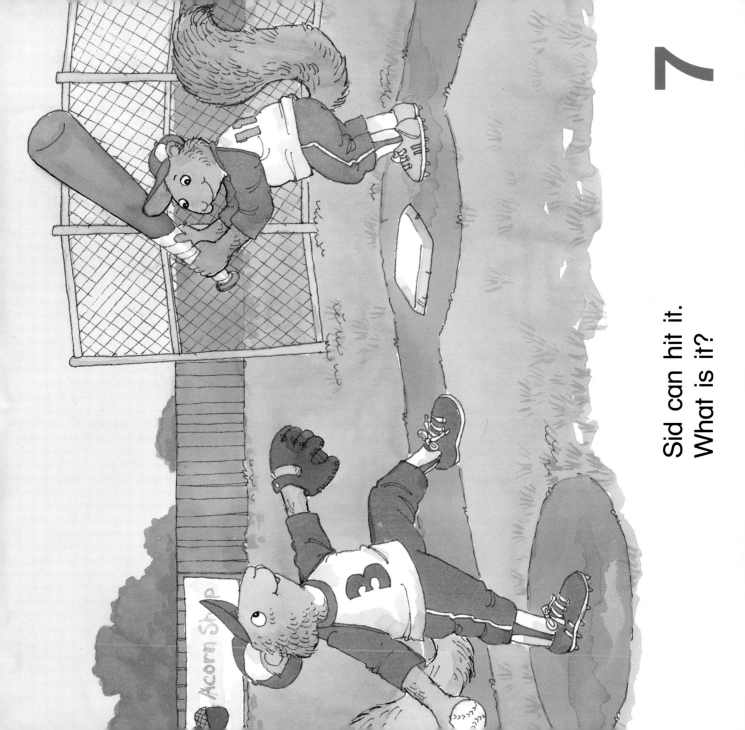

7

Sid can hit it.
What is it?

Sid can win it.
What is it?

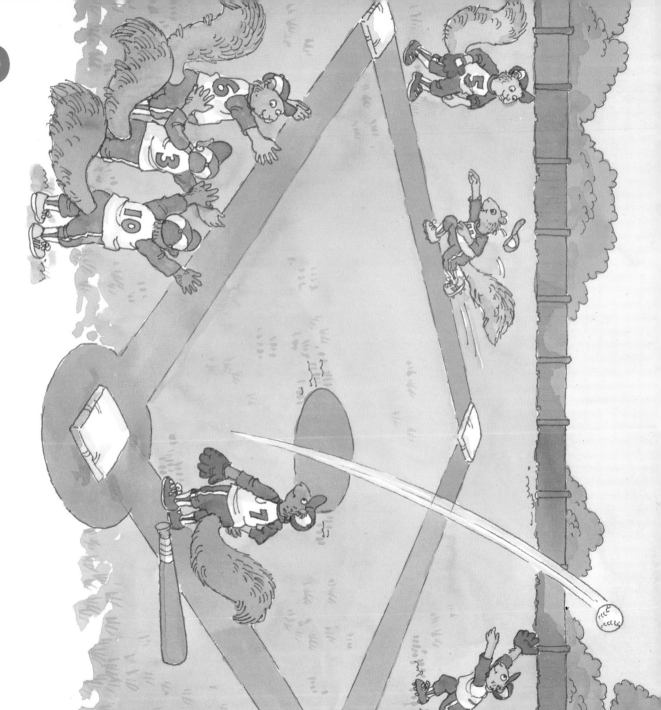